AR 1.2/ . 5

Guess What

Published in the United States of America by
Cherry Lake Publishing
Ann Arbor, Michigan
www.cherrylakepublishing.com

Content Adviser: Susan Heinrichs Gray
Reading Adviser: Marla Conn, ReadAbility, Inc.
Book Designer: Felicia Macheske

Photo Credits: © Mr. SUTTIPON YAKHAM/Shutterstock Images, cover; © Sebastian Janicki/Shutterstock Images, 1, 4; © Pan Xunbin/Shutterstock Images, 3; © niceregionpics/Shutterstock Images, 7; © Laura Bartlett/Shutterstock Images, 8; © Vitalii Hulai/ Shutterstock Images, 11; © paulrommerShutterstock Images, 12; © LorraineHudgins/Shutterstock Images, 14; © phichit Bhumadhana/Shutterstock Images, 17; © Ekaterina Pankina/Shutterstock Images, 18;© Hintau Aliaksei/Shutterstock Images, 21; © Andrey_Kuzmin/Shutterstock Images, back cover; © Eric Isselee/Shutterstock Images, back cover

Library of Congress Cataloging-in-Publication Data

Macheske, Felicia, author.
 Quick and quiet : dragonfly / Felicia Macheske.
 pages cm. — (Guess what)
 Summary: "Young children are natural problem solvers and always looking for answers, especially when it involves interesting insects. Guess What: Quick and Quiet: Dragonfly provides young curious readers with striking visual clues and simply written hints. Using the photos and text, readers rely on visual literacy skills, reading, and reasoning as they solve the insect mystery. Clearly written facts give readers a deeper understanding of how the insect lives. Additional text features, including a glossary and an index, help students locate information and learn new words"— Provided by publisher.
 Audience: K to grade 3.
 Includes index.
 ISBN 978-1-63470-715-2 (hardcover) — ISBN 978-1-63470-745-9 (pbk.) — ISBN 978-1-63470-730-5 (pdf) — ISBN 978-1-63470-760-2 (ebook)
 1. Dragonflies—Juvenile literature. 2. Children's questions and answers. I. Title.
 QL520.M32 2016
 595.7'33—dc23
 2015026088

Cherry Lake Publishing would like to acknowledge the work of The Partnership for 21st Century Skills.
Please visit *www.p21.org* for more information.

Printed in the United States of America
Corporate Graphics

Table of Contents

I have eyes that can see all around me.

My four wings can each move in a different direction.

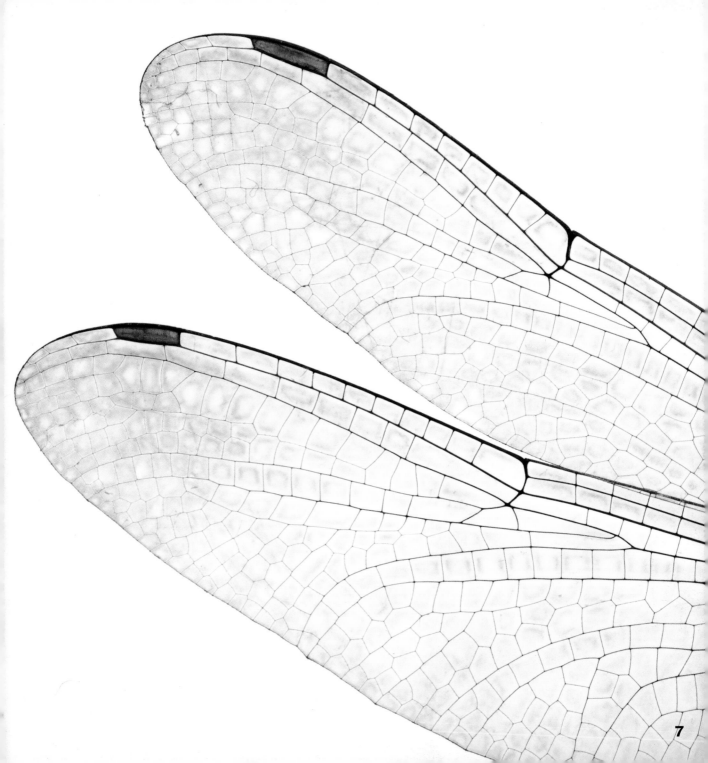

7

I live near lakes and streams.

I live in the water when I am young.

I can
be very
colorful.

13

I eat other insects and spiders.

And other animals might eat me too.

Oh no!

Some people think I look like a helicopter.

Do you know what I am?

I'm a Dragonfly!

About Dragonflies

1. Dragonflies are very hard to catch. That's partly because of their ability to see in all directions.

2. Young dragonflies are called **nymphs**.

3. Dragonflies have been around for over 250 million years.

4. Some dragonflies fly long distances to **migrate**.

5. A dragonfly's four wings allow it to change direction quickly.

Glossary

helicopter (HEL-ih-kahp-tur) an aircraft with large, spinning blades on top and no wings

insects (IN-sekts) small animals with no backbone, six legs, and three main body sections

migrate (MYE-grate) to move from one area to another

nymphs (NIMFS) a name used for some insects, such as dragonflies, that have not yet become adults

Index